GW00778273

NO.

DAVID MICHAELI

NO.

ASTROLOG PUBLISHERS

DAVID MICHAELI
NO.

© 1997 by Astrolog Publishers

Published by: Astrolog Publishers,
P.O.B. 1123,
Hod Hasharon 45111, Israel,
TEL/FAX. 972-9-7412044

ISBN 965-494-002-7

Printed in Israel.

Introduction

"No" is not a negative word. It is protective, safeguarding, defining and discerning. We acknowledge ourselves through the word "no." We can intensify and sharpen things with a "no," while remaining level-headed enough to focus our minds on the issue.

"No" is a signal word. After the magic word "no" has shed light on the possibilities facing us, we become more certain of the correct thing to do. The word "no" is liberating. It releases us from the burden of unnecessary, and improper actions and feelings. Are we ready to accept the gift inherent in the word "no"?

NO,

this isn't your house.

You must find one of your own.

9

NO,

this isn't your line of work.

You must choose your own

line of work.

NO,

manners can't take the place of
decisions.

You must decide.

NO,

fear isn't a good adviser, but a bad one.
Go against it.

NO,

anger doesn't clarify your feelings,

it obscures them.

You must express your feelings clearly.

17

NO,

you don't need to invest work in a place
where you aren't wanted.
You must go to a place where you
are wanted.

NO,

using someone else's words won't get you what he got.

You must formulate your own words.

NO,

using someone else's customs won't get you what he got.

You must create your own private customs.

NO,

24

the doctor isn't always right.

You must ask another doctor.

NO,

the teacher isn't always right.

You must ask yourself.

NO,

the bus driver isn't always careful.

You must always check the change.

NO,

the salesperson's smile is not honest.
You must consider the offer while
ignoring the smile.

NO,

this isn't the last chance.

There's always something else.

33

NO,

this isn't the end.

Another opportunity always arises

in the end.

NO,

the teacher isn't thinking of your good.

He's building himself through you.

37

NO,

the teacher isn't an enemy.

You take things from him for a price.

NO,

being exploited isn't bad.

It shows you have something to give.

NO,

absolute generosity isn't good.

You must keep enough to be able

to give.

NO,

an injury isn't bad luck.

It's a junction in your life that might be

rescuing you from other trouble.

NO,

rejection doesn't disqualify you

as a person.

It can be a test of your resilience.

NO,

assets don't make you happy.

You must find yourself despite your
assets.

NO,

money isn't a solution to anxiety.
Anxiety is a separate problem that you
must solve.

51

NO,

money doesn't solve emotional
problems - it covers them.
You must solve them despite the
money.

NO,

54

medication isn't a solution to anxiety.
Anxiety is an inner problem that you
must solve.

55

NO,

escape isn't a solution to anxiety.

Anxiety is the motivation for escape.

NO,

poverty isn't romantic.

You must find a way to live at peace
with yourself.

NO,

being nice is prostitution.

You must express your will clearly.

NO,

judging yourself isn't an admirable trait,
you must accept yourself.
Self-judgment enables others to
pronounce an even harsher sentence
on you.

NO,

cynicism is not maturity.

You must be empathetic.

65

NO,

orderliness is not learned.

It's an expression of your inner order.

NO,

quoting sayings and observing customs

don't show your wisdom.

You must relinquish quotations;

they mask fear.

69

NO,

openness isn't safe.

Openness is an adventure.

NO,

behaving nicely isn't nice.

It's fear of the other person's reaction.

NO,

this isn't your life.

You must create your own.

75

NO,

endurance isn't a positive attribute.

You must stop being a victim.

NO,

restraint isn't a positive attribute.

You must stop being a martyr.

NO,

the media don't tell you the truth.

They build an imaginary reality.

NO,

the products you use aren't safe.

Carefully choose the ones that are safer.

NO,

your current way of life isn't the
only one.

There are many other possibilities.

NO,

absolute despair and a distinct feeling
of loss and futility, aren't cause
for suicide.

They signify a new beginning.

NO,

work isn't holy.

If you stop working you won't die.

NO,

age isn't an impediment.

Today's fashion of youth is changing.

NO,

changing direction in life doesn't
indicate instability.

It shows you're still alive.

NO,

age isn't an impediment.

You must recognize your true,

ageless self.

NO,

you can't plan for a second time around in life.

You must realize your potential now.

NO,

medicine isn't absolute.

It varies according to fashion.

NO,

you aren't being punished your

whole life.

You deserve to be treated fairly.

NO,

nothing justifies unbalanced

relationships.

NO,

104

nothing justifies an imbalance between work and its remuneration.

NO,

letting people lean on you isn't an act of kindness but exploitation of their weakness.

NO,

you don't have to be alone.

You must understand that every person
who connects with you in any way -
needs you.

NO,

the pain in your heart isn't punishment. You must recognize it as the feeling of your life and go with it.

NO,

you can't receive.

You must give in order to receive.

NO,

not knowing isn't a disgrace.

It's honest.

NO,

what you see isn't reality but a

projection of your inner image.

NO,

118

your thoughts are not your own.

They're a reflection of external data

and aren't always true.

NO,

120

money and assets aren't tangible.

Money and assets are religion.

NO,

that isn't an enemy.

That's another person.

NO,

a child isn't half a person,

he's a whole person.

NO,

turning your back on the problem isn't

a solution but a deferment.

You must address the problem itself.

NO,

you aren't a mistake.

You have a place in the world and

you must take it.

NO,

ideology isn't sacrifice but an ego trip.

131

NO,

you don't have to suffer in order

to receive.

You should recognize that.

NO,

self-pity isn't worth anything.

It's a dead-end street.

NO,

fatigue in life isn't objective.

It's means you're not interested in what you're doing.

you're doing.

NO,

boredom isn't objective.

It means you're closed off to what's

happening around you.

NO,

140

taking an interest in someone because of their possessions isn't real interest. It's nullification of that person.

NO,

having both feet on the ground means
being stuck.
You must pick up one foot in order to
move forward.

NO,

a place isn't an inanimate thing that you can exploit, pollute, and ignore.

You must treat it with the respect it deserves, or it will harm you.

NO,

you aren't a soldier of profession.

You are a free person.

NO,

you aren't a soldier of manners.

You are a free person.

NO,

you aren't a prisoner of habit.

You are a free person.

NO,

you aren't a decoration.

Don't go where they don't want

contact with you.

153

NO,

154

you aren't a nuisance.

Don't go where they don't want

contact with you.

NO,

you aren't a poor wretch.

Don't go where they don't want

contact with you.

NO,

you aren't unusual.

You're afraid of establishing contact.

NO,

you aren't unusual.

Everyone is afraid of establishing

contact.

NO,

gifts aren't always an expression

of care.

They're often bribes.

NO,

you didn't forget. You stole.

NO,

you didn't forget. You were neglectful.

NO,

being miserable doesn't require
participation. Quite the contrary.
The more you participate, the more
miserable you'll be.

NO,

addiction of any kind isn't an external
thing but an inner weakness.
The more you lend support to an addict,
the more you'll feed his inner weakness.

NO,

addiction isn't an external thing.

I must recognize my weakness in order to get rid of it.

NO,

violence isn't a personality trait.

It's a distortion of the desire for contact.

NO,

love isn't limited by any

particular terms.

You must love unconditionally.

NO,

love isn't a means of control.

You must acknowledge the existence of others.

NO,

love isn't a pact for improving the race.
You must acknowledge the existence
of others.

NO,

light-skinned people aren't cleaner than dark-skinned people.

NO,

dark-skinned people aren't more dangerous than light-skinned people.

NO,

you don't do anything for your beloved. You do it for yourself.

NO,

you don't do anything for your country. You do it for yourself.

NO,

190

you don't do anything for your god.
You do it for yourself.

NO,

the commercials don't want you.

They want your money.

NO,

your child will never fulfill your image.
He has to fulfill himself.

NO,

beauty doesn't promise a proper life.

You must do it yourself.

NO,

nothing is eternal.

Everything ends just as it began.

NO,

200

your body isn't eternal.

You must acknowledge natural change.

NO,

there's no reward whatsoever for understanding.

Except taking advantage of the situation.

NO,

there's no reward whatsoever for

understanding, for suffering, for

sacrifice.

These are your choices.

NO,

disability doesn't hurt your soul.

That's your choice.

NO,

children aren't more resilient
than adults.

209

NO,

your inner voice never lies.

You should listen to it.

211

your inner voice never lies.

You should listen to it.

NO,

you aren't alone in the world. That's a
spoiled, cowardly attitude.
You must dare to meet others.

NO,

the pain of children isn't smaller than
the pain of adults.
Children are just more helpless.

NO,

216

taking action isn't always the right thing to do.

NO,

consistency isn't always a positive trait.
Sometimes it expresses an addiction.

NO,

responsibility isn't always

a positive trait.

Sometimes it's an expression of fear.

NO,

trying to act grown-up when you're

young is not right.

You must live your young life in full;

only then can you mature.

NO,

being a good kid won't get you anything, but will only enable your environment to do whatever it wants with you.

You must be yourself.

NO,

faith and religion aren't a spiritual

solution.

They're an organizational solution.

NO,

solitude doesn't mean being alone.

It means recognizing your independent

existence as a living, feeling creature

within the creation.

NO,

you can't give indiscriminately and boundlessly.

You must ration your giving so it won't dry up.

NO,

stealing isn't a conscious thing.

Stealing is survival.

It means - I think I don't deserve
anything.

NO,

a mental handicap isn't abstract and
invisible.

It's a handicap to all intents and
purposes.

NO,

I don't exist alone in universe.

I belong to the pattern of the

human continuum.

NO,

touching others doesn't harm me. Touching is part of my physical and mental health.

NO,

240

love doesn't come out of the blue.

Love is a decision.

NO.